PSALM 145

WRITTEN BY
BEATRICE FISHBACK
ELIZABETH TYRRELL

Published by Military Ministry Press, a ministry of Cru Military, 100 Lake Hart Dr, Orlando, FL 32832. 1.800.444.6006 www.crumilitary.org

Scripture quotations are from The Holy Bible, English Standard Version© (ESV©), copyright © 2001 by Crossway, a publishing ministry of Good News Publishers. Used by permission. All rights reserved.

Acknowledgements:
Gabrielle Mattingly: kid-consultant
Ashley Bowron Peterson: graphic artist

Published in the United States of America
ISBN 978-0-98448-548-2

QUEST

A SEEKING: A JOURNEY IN SEARCH OF ADVENTURE

While you wait for your dad or mom to return from a deployment—a journey to another land—you are on a journey also. But your journey is different. It can be a QUEST to find God in your everyday life, to become closer to Him, to be His friend and to know He is yours.

Here are a few things you can do to make it easier for you during the deployment:

- Talk to your parents and share with them your thoughts and feelings.

- Talk to other kids who are going through the same thing and try to help each other.

- Talk to God and tell Him how you feel.

You can be totally real with God. He can help you through this time because He knows everything, and He knows everything about you. And He loves you!

Sometimes it helps to write things down—to get it out in the open. You can use this little booklet of prayers and journaling space as a guide. Each day offers:

- an alphabetized word from Psalm 145.

- a QUESTion to help you focus your attention on God, how good He is, and how you can rely on Him.

This will help take your mind off your fears about this deployment. Remember, you can depend on God. He is walking beside you on this amazing QUEST.

I will extol you, my God and King, and bless your name
forever and ever.

Every day I will bless you and praise your name forever
and ever.

Great is the Lord, and greatly to be praised, and his
greatness is unsearchable.

One generation shall commend your works to another,
and shall declare your mighty acts.

On the glorious splendor of your majesty, and on your
wondrous works, I will meditate.

They shall speak of the might of your awesome deeds, and
I will declare your greatness.

They shall pour forth the fame of your abundant
goodness and shall sing aloud of your righteousness.

The Lord is gracious and merciful, slow to anger and
abounding in steadfast love.

The Lord is good to all, and his mercy is over all that he
has made.

All your works shall give thanks to You, O Lord, and all
your saints shall bless you!

They shall speak of the glory of your kingdom and tell of
your power,

to make known to the children of man your mighty deeds,
and the glorious splendor of your kingdom.

Your kingdom is an everlasting kingdom, and your
dominion endures throughout all generations.

[The Lord is faithful in all his words and kind in all his
works.]

The Lord upholds all who are falling and raises up all who
are bowed down.

The eyes of all look to you, and you give them their food
in due season.

You open your hand; you satisfy the desire of every living
thing.

The Lord is righteous in all his ways and kind in all his
works.

The Lord is near to all who call on him, to all who call on
him in truth.

He fulfills the desire of those who fear him; he also hears
their cry and saves them.

The Lord preserves all who love him, but all the wicked
he will destroy.

My mouth will speak the praise of the Lord, and let all
flesh bless his holy name forever and ever.

PSALM 145

BEGIN YOUR QUEST ...

Awesome: totally cool

Prayer: God, I never really thought about 'awesome' as a word to describe You. My friends talk about their iPhones being awesome or a team being great. But You are Awesome above everything and everyone else. You are so great. You even know everything about me and how I worry about my parents. When they are gone, I feel scared, but You remind me today that You are Awesome, and You don't want me to be worried. Thanks for being who You are and for caring so much for me during this time.

In Jesus' Name, Amen.

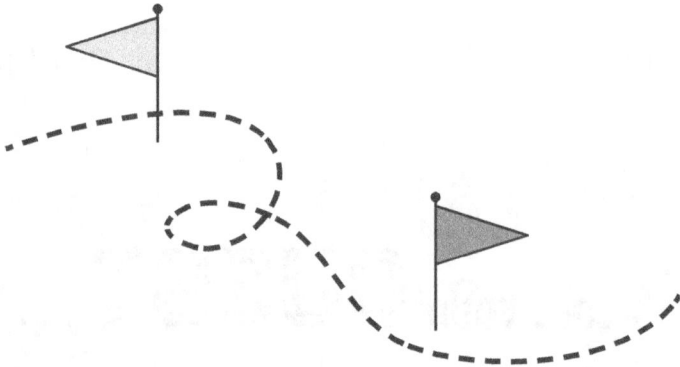

QUESTion: How is God Awesome in your life, even in the middle of this deployment?

_____

_____

_____

_____

_____

_____

_____

_____

_____

_____

_____

_____

_____

_____

_____

"They shall speak of the might of your awesome deeds."
Psalm 145:6a

BLESS: TO APPRECIATE; TO BE GRATEFUL

Prayer: God, when my parents thank me for doing something for them, it shows they're grateful, not just because of what I did but because they appreciate who I am. When I pray and say thanks, it shows I appreciate You and am thankful for who You are too. So thank you, God, for doing so many great things for me, for giving me everything and everyone I love. Thank you for doing a good job of taking care of me. Because You have already done so many great things, I know You will even take care of me when my dad or mom is deployed. Thank You.

In Jesus' Name, Amen.

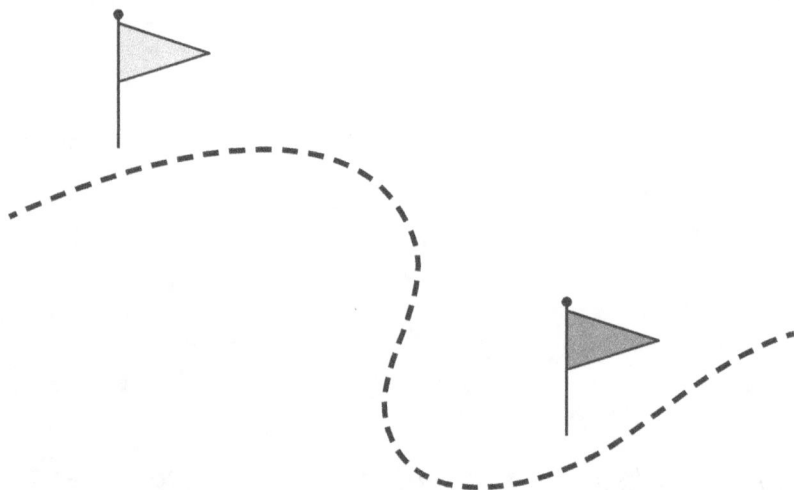

QUESTion: Even though deployment is difficult, what are you grateful for during this time?

_____

_____

_____

_____

_____

_____

_____

_____

_____

_____

_____

_____

_____

_____

_____

_____

_____

_____

"Every day I will bless you." Psalm 145:2a

C

COMMEND: TO PRAISE; COMPLIMENT

Prayer: God, I like it when others say nice things about me. When friends or my parents compliment me, it makes me want to do more for them. I need to remember to say good things about You, too. I can tell my friends how great You are. I can tell them how much I appreciate all You do for my family and me. Help me to remember today to say good things about You to others. This will take my mind off how hard this deployment can be and also off myself.

In Jesus' Name, Amen.

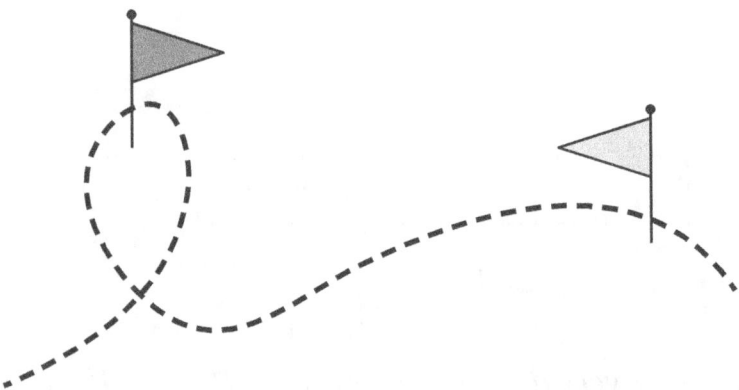

QUESTion: What good things has God done in your life? Tell someone.

_____

_____

_____

_____

_____

_____

_____

_____

_____

_____

_____

_____

_____

_____

_____

_____

_____

"One generation shall commend your works to another, and shall declare your mighty acts." Psalm 145:4

DOMINION: TOTAL RULE

Prayer: God, dominion is a word that simply means You control all. You have control in heaven and on earth. Everything belongs to You: the birds in the sky, the fish in the ocean. You are in charge of the stars and the sea, the major and the minor. Thank You, God, that Your dominion includes me. You know where I am right this minute, and You know where my dad or mom is too. It makes me feel safe just knowing You are in charge of each one of us.

In Jesus' Name, Amen.

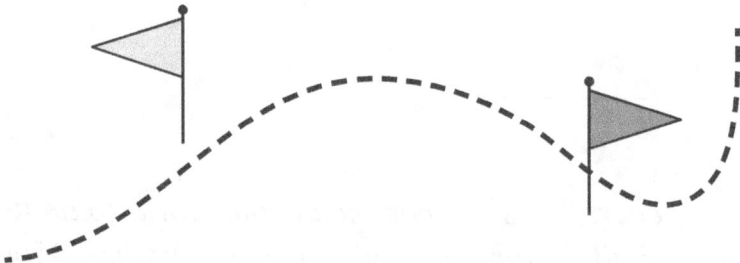

QUESTion: How do you feel knowing God is in control?

_____

_____

_____

_____

_____

_____

_____

_____

_____

_____

_____

_____

_____

_____

_____

_____

_____

*"Your kingdom is an everlasting kingdom, and your
dominion endures throughout all generations."*
Psalm 145:13

Exalt: to make more important than anything else

Prayer: God, worship is one way we can show that You are more important than anything else, and we can worship You in many ways. When we sing in church, we are worshipping You, and when we get down on our knees and pray, that's worship too. When I am thankful for things that happen during the day, that's also a way of worshipping You. Help me today to be thankful for things even when I can't think of something to thank You for. Maybe I can start by thanking You for small things like having a bed to sleep in. I want to learn how to worship You with my thanks.

In Jesus' Name, Amen.

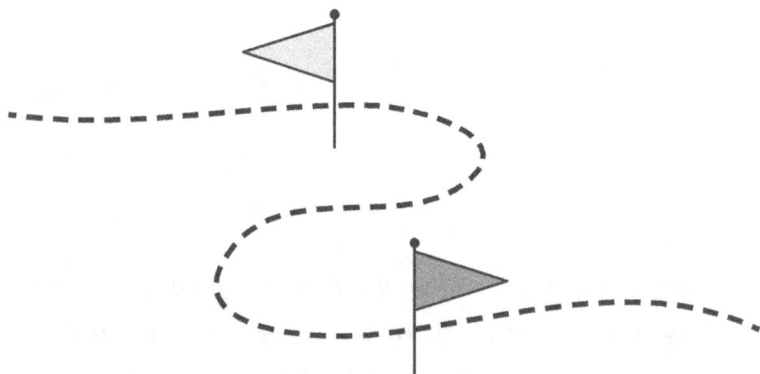

QUESTion: What ten things can you thank God for today?

_____

_____

_____

_____

_____

_____

_____

_____

_____

_____

_____

_____

_____

_____

_____

_____

_____

_____

*"...to make known to the children of man
your mighty deeds." Psalm 145:12a*

F FOREVER: FOR ALL FUTURE TIME; FOR ALWAYS

Prayer: God, forever is so hard to figure out. I think of forever as being all the days before I was born and all the days from now on. The Bible says You have been here forever. You lived before everything was made, and You will still be around even when everything is gone. I can feel safe because You will be with me today, tomorrow, and the next day. I don't ever have to worry about feeling alone because You are right here, right now. Thanks for letting me know I can count on You to be around even when my dad or mom is away.

In Jesus' Name, Amen.

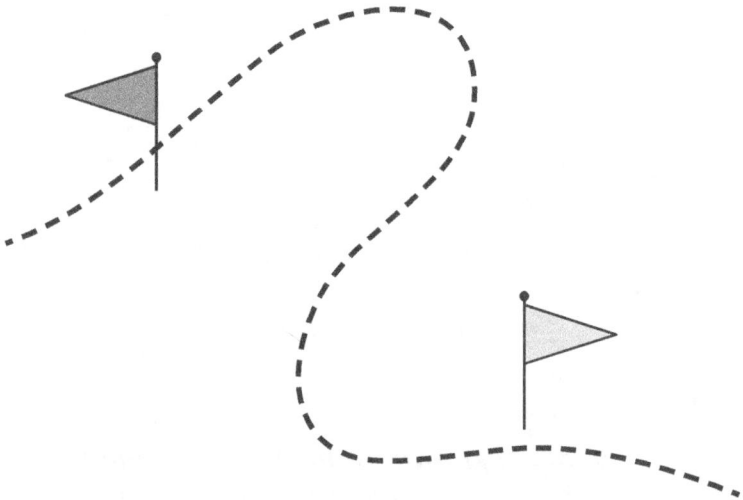

QUESTion: What does forever mean to you?

_____

_____

_____

_____

_____

_____

_____

_____

_____

_____

_____

_____

_____

_____

_____

_____

_____

_____

_____

_____

"...and bless your name forever and ever." Psalm 145:1b

G GREATNESS: IMPORTANCE; FAME

Prayer: God, I like some people I see on TV. I think it's because they are famous and important. But You are the greatest! You are greater than anyone on television or in movies because YOU made everything, You own everything, and You're way more famous than any of them. So that's really what I need to remember when I see others and how famous they are. Sometimes I want to be like them. Instead, I should want to be more like You.

In Jesus' Name, Amen.

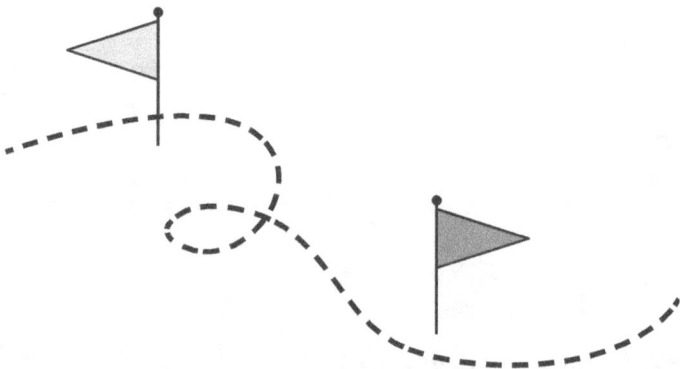

QUESTion: What do you think is great about God?

_____
_____
_____
_____
_____
_____
_____
_____
_____
_____
_____
_____
_____
_____
_____
_____
_____

"Great is the Lord, and greatly to be praised, and his greatness is unsearchable." Psalm 145:3

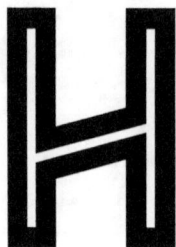

H **HOLY: WITHOUT SIN; PURE**

Prayer: God, I know sin is doing something wrong. One way I sin is by disobeying my parents. Another way is by not listening to my teachers. How is it possible to be without sin, to be sin-less, to never do anything wrong? Only Jesus was perfect and was sin-less. I know I can't ever be perfect. That's why I need You to be in my heart. You are the only one who can help me choose to do the right things when my dad or mom is deployed.

In Jesus' Name, Amen.

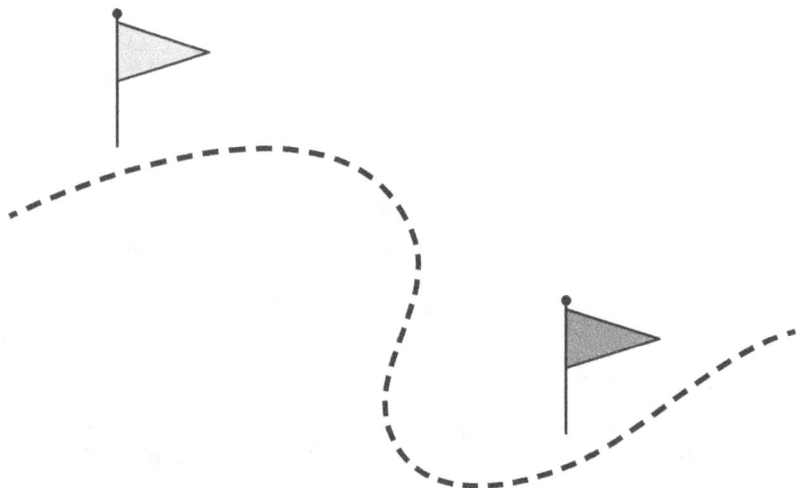

QUESTion: What does it mean to let Jesus live in your heart?

_____

_____

_____

_____

_____

_____

_____

_____

_____

_____

_____

_____

_____

_____

_____

_____

"...and let all flesh bless his holy name forever and ever."
Psalm 145:21b

I WILL: TO DO THE THINGS GOD ASKS US TO DO

Prayer: God, You ask me to be kind to others, love those who don't like me, and love You with my whole heart. Doing these things means I am being obedient. But a lot of times I am disobedient. I don't do what my parents ask even though I say I will. If I learn to obey You, maybe it will be easier to obey my parents, especially when one of them is deployed. Please help me to be obedient.

In Jesus' Name, Amen.

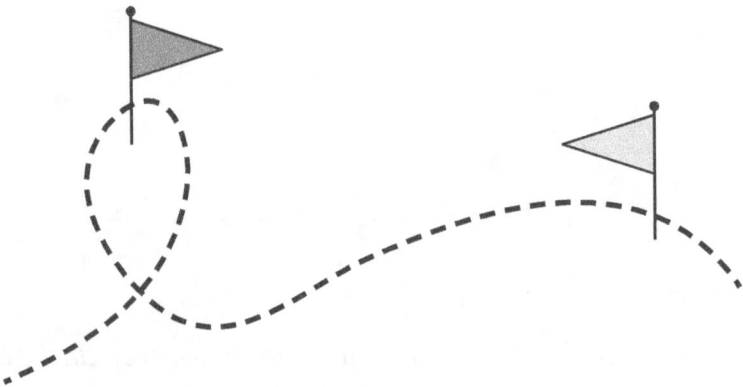

QUESTion: What are some things you can do today to show God you are willing to obey Him?

_____

_____

_____

_____

_____

_____

_____

_____

_____

_____

_____

_____

_____

_____

_____

_____

_____

"...I will declare your greatness." Psalm 145:6b

J JOYFUL: MAJORLY HAPPY

Prayer: God, I can't help being worried or afraid when my dad or mom is away. It makes me sad sometimes when I can't see him or her. Yet, You want me to be joyful and happy although my parent is deployed. It's better for me to think about the joy You give me even when things are not easy. I know You can help me see things Your way and have joy when I don't feel it. Help me to have Your joy today.

In Jesus' Name, Amen.

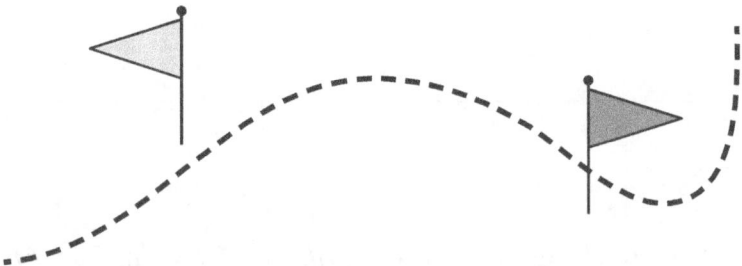

QUESTion: Why do you think God wants us to be joyful even when we don't feel like it?

_____

_____

_____

_____

_____

_____

_____

_____

_____

_____

_____

_____

_____

_____

_____

[With great joy] "My mouth will speak the praise of the Lord." Psalm 145:21a

K

KINGDOM: EVERYTHING BELONGS TO GOD

Prayer: God, I've read stories about knights and kings like King Arthur. They live in castles and ride on horses. But there is another kingdom I can't see with my eyes. It's Your kingdom in heaven. You have angels who live with You in Your kingdom, and You also reign over the kingdom of the world I can see. You know what's going on everywhere, all the time. This means You are in charge where my dad or mom is and know exactly what is happening with him or her. That gives me peace. Thank You. In Jesus' Name, Amen.

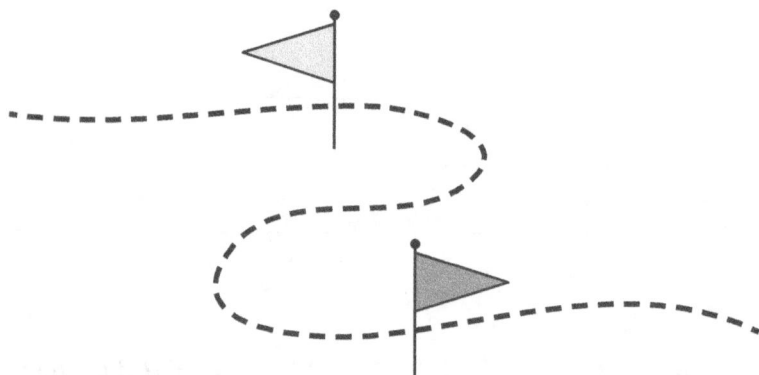

QUESTion: What does "God's kingdom" mean to you?

_____

_____

_____

_____

_____

_____

_____

_____

_____

_____

_____

_____

_____

_____

_____

_____

_____

"They shall speak of the glory of your kingdom, and tell of your power." Psalm 145:11

LORD: GOD

Prayer: God, You are the creator—that means You made everything. You are the ruler of the universe—that means You rule the whole wide world and even worlds we can't see. You are the source of all power. You are like all the superheroes of the world rolled into one. You have total power, total control, everywhere and in every place. You know the smallest thing I have in my heart, and I can trust You to take care of me when I feel lonely or scared. Thank You for loving me so much.

In Jesus' Name, Amen.

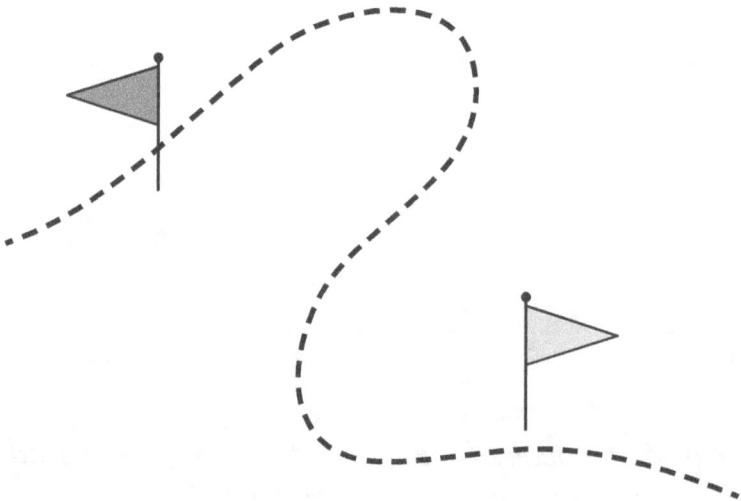

QUESTion: How does it make you feel knowing that God is all-powerful?

_____

_____

_____

_____

_____

_____

_____

_____

_____

_____

_____

_____

_____

_____

"The Lord is good to all." Psalm 145:9a

m MERCIFUL: TO SHOW KINDNESS WHEN SOMEONE HURTS

Prayer: God, if I looked in the dictionary, I would read that merciful means helping someone when something bad is going on, like a doctor or nurse taking care of a person who is sick. When I see my friends hurting because someone did something to them or because their parents are deployed, I want to help my friends. Help me know when my friends need me and help me to share Your love.

In Jesus' Name, Amen.

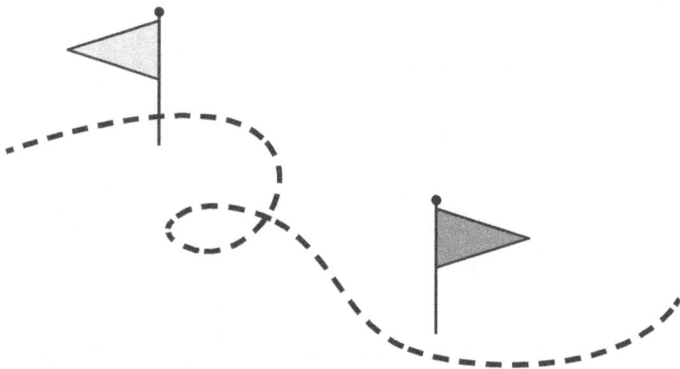

QUESTion: Do you have friends you can help? How can you show them God's love?

_____

_____

_____

_____

_____

_____

_____

_____

_____

_____

_____

_____

_____

_____

_____

_____

"The Lord is gracious and merciful, slow to anger and abounding in steadfast love." Psalm 145:8

N

NEAR: CLOSE BY

Prayer: God, if I put my hand in front of my face in the dark, even though I can't see it, I know my hand is there. You are like that. I can't see You, but You are near. When I walk to school, You are right next to me. When I eat my meals, You sit close by. Even though I can't touch or see You, You've told me in the Bible that You will never leave me. If I pray in my heart, wherever I am, I know You will hear me because You are as close to me as my hand. Thank You for being so near.

In Jesus' Name, Amen.

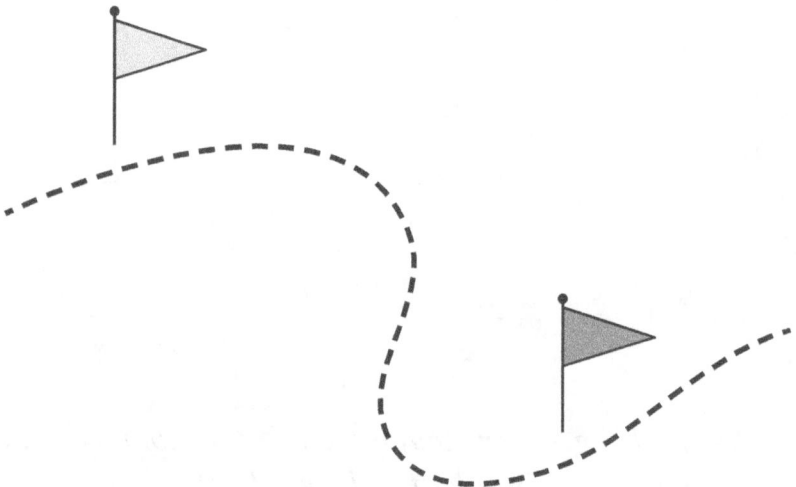

QUESTion: How does knowing that God is near help you when you are afraid?

_____

_____

_____

_____

_____

_____

_____

_____

_____

_____

_____

_____

_____

_____

_____

_____

_____

_____

"The Lord is near to all who call on him, to all who call on him in truth." Psalm 145:18

O ONE: SINGLE

Prayer: God, there is only One God—You. You don't want me to treat other things more importantly than You. It's okay for me to like my iPhone or my computer or my television. It's okay to want to hang out with my friends or talk on the phone. But sometimes when I do those things, I forget about You. Help me to remember You are more important than anything or anyone else, and no matter what I'm doing, I can stop and say thanks. That's all it takes to let You know how important You are to me.

In Jesus' Name, Amen.

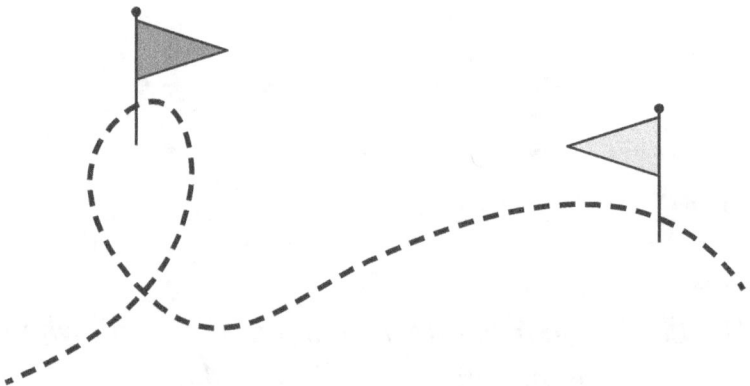

QUESTion: What are you making more important in your life than God?

_____

_____

_____

_____

_____

_____

_____

_____

_____

_____

_____

_____

_____

_____

_____

"One generation shall commend your works to another, and shall declare your mighty acts." Psalm 145:4

P PRAISE: TO CELEBRATE

Prayer: God, I can't wait until it's my birthday. I might get gifts or have some friends over for a party. My parents make a big deal when it's my birthday, and that makes me feel pretty special. I guess praising You is like that. It's having a big party, and You are the one we are celebrating! You don't need any gifts because You have everything. But my parents tell me You like it when we sing to You, pray to You, or tell others about You. Praising You doesn't cost me anything. Even if my dad or mom is deployed and I don't feel like celebrating, I need to remember to praise You in some way each day.

In Jesus' Name, Amen.

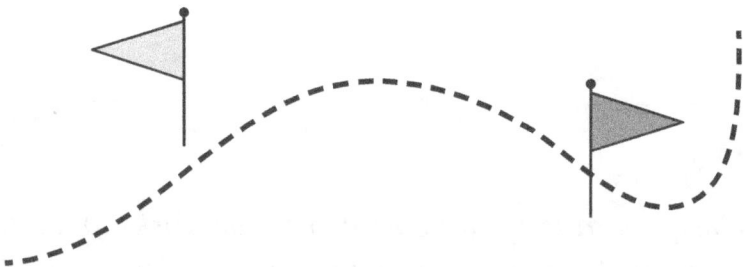

QUESTion: How can you show God today that
He is special to you?

_____

_____

_____

_____

_____

_____

_____

_____

_____

_____

_____

_____

_____

_____

_____

"...and praise your name forever and ever."
Psalm 145:2b

QUALITY: SUPER GOOD; EXCELLENT

Prayer: God, You are excellent, but I just can't help thinking this deployment is not fair! I miss talking and having fun with my dad or mom. Somehow it's wrong that we're apart. I can't figure out how that can be good. Skype and email just aren't the same as having my dad or mom at home with me. I guess I just need to trust You and remember You are super good even in the middle of hard stuff. Please help me today when I'm upset about my dad or mom being away.

In Jesus' Name, Amen.

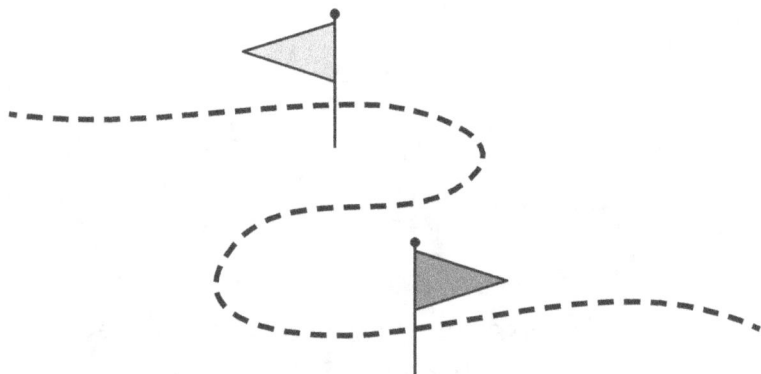

QUESTion: In what ways is God good even though this deployment is hard for me?

_____

_____

_____

_____

_____

_____

_____

_____

_____

_____

_____

_____

_____

_____

_____

_____

"The Lord is good to all." Psalm 145:9a

R RIGHTEOUS: GOOD; HONEST

Prayer: God, You are so good, and I want to be good as well. Being good means doing what I know is right and not letting my friends talk me into doing something wrong, so I get into trouble and disappoint my parents. I want other kids to look at me and see a good person not a troublemaker. I need You to help me do the right things so that You and my parents are proud of me. Please help me today to think first before I say or do anything that might make others unhappy.

In Jesus' Name, Amen.

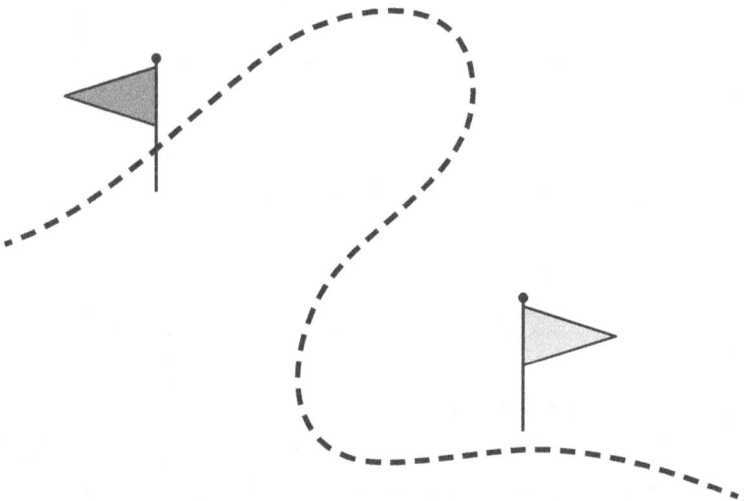

QUESTion: What will you say if your friends ask you to do something wrong?

_____

_____

_____

_____

_____

_____

_____

_____

_____

_____

_____

_____

_____

_____

_____

_____

"The Lord is righteous in all his ways and kind in all his works." Psalm 145:17

S SPLENDOR: BEAUTY

Prayer: God, splendor means beauty. If I take the time to think about all the things that are beautiful, it reminds me that You must be beautiful too. A lot of times I don't think about what is beautiful because I'm feeling sad. Nothing seems fair and I don't feel happy. But if I stopped and thought about one thing that is nice, it would make me feel so much better. Please open my eyes today to one nice thing that is beautiful, one thing that makes me think of You and see Your beauty.

In Jesus' Name, Amen.

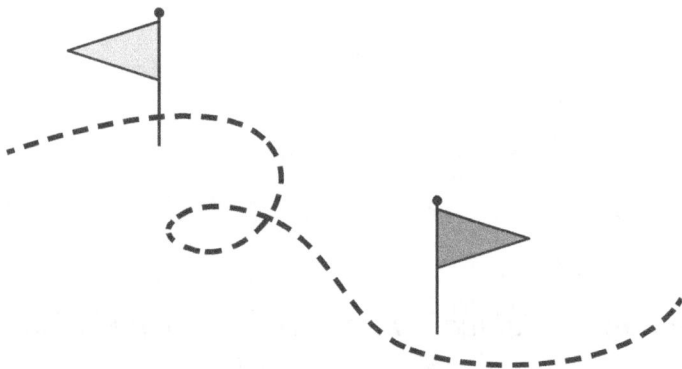

QUESTion: What have you seen today that reminds you of how beautiful God is?

_____

_____

_____

_____

_____

_____

_____

_____

_____

_____

_____

_____

_____

_____

_____

"...the glorious splendor of your kingdom."
Psalm 145:12b

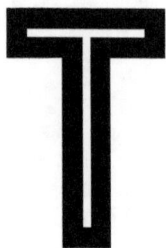

T TRUTH: HONESTY

Prayer: God, sometimes it's really easy to tell a lie. I think I need to lie in order to get my own way or to be accepted or to have an easy way out of a bad place. You don't tell any lies. You don't 'stretch' the truth to get Your own way or to be accepted. The next time I want to tell a lie, please help me remember this will not make You happy. Instead I can pray to You and ask You to help me tell the truth. I want to be an example to others of how You want me to behave.

In Jesus' Name, Amen.

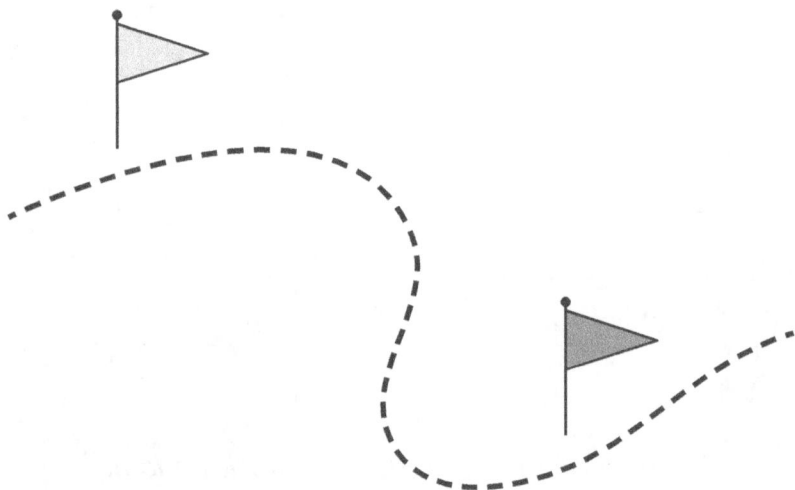

QUESTion: When are you tempted to lie?
How can praying to God help you tell the truth?

_____

_____

_____

_____

_____

_____

_____

_____

_____

_____

_____

_____

_____

_____

_____

_____

"The Lord is near to all who call on him, to all who call on him in truth." Psalm 145:18

UPHOLDS: DEFENDS; PROTECTS

Prayer: God, the military protects us from others who don't understand our way of life. My dad or mom is deployed and is defending our country from people who might want to hurt us. God, You are like that. You protect me and keep me safe from others who want to hurt me with words or actions. Not everyone is nice and not everyone gets along, but I need to remember no matter what others say or do, You are here with me. I can rely on You to protect me. Thank You.

In Jesus' Name, Amen.

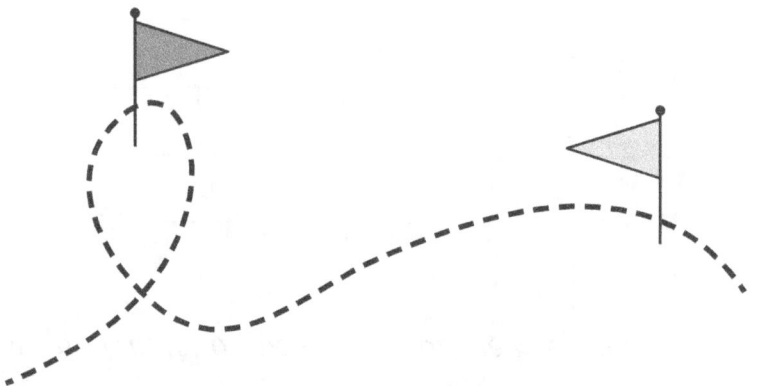

QUESTion: How has God protected you from mean people? Give an example.

_____

_____

_____

_____

_____

_____

_____

_____

_____

_____

_____

_____

_____

_____

_____

_____

"The Lord upholds all who are falling." Psalm 145:14a

V

eVERLASTING: NEVER ENDING

Prayer: God, my day starts when I get out of bed, and my day ends when I go to bed and sleep. My parents tell me I need sleep to stay healthy and strong. They want me to stay well so they won't worry when they are deployed. But God, You don't need rest. You don't need sleep. You are awake and take care of me even when I'm sleeping. Your care for me never ends: morning, noon or night. Thank You. I can depend on You, anytime and for all time—even when I am grown up.

In Jesus' Name, Amen.

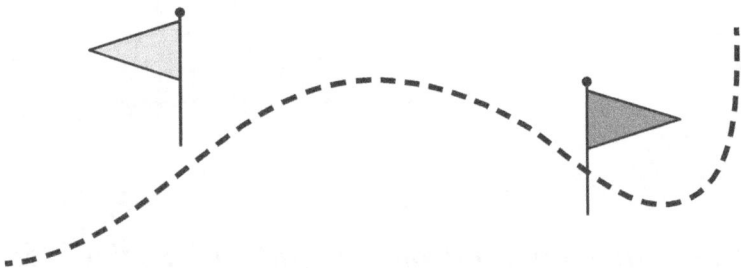

QUESTion: How does knowing God is always there help you?

_____

_____

_____

_____

_____

_____

_____

_____

_____

_____

_____

_____

_____

_____

_____

_____

"Your kingdom is an everlasting kingdom."
Psalm 145:13a

WONDROUS: SURPRISINGLY GREAT

Prayer: God, I feel great when I go with my family on vacation. We get to see and do fun things. It's a wonderful feeling to be together as a family and do stuff—even if it's something small like a picnic or something big like a trip to another place. It's an adventure. Right now we can't do this, but I can look forward to the time when my dad or mom is home again, and our family can go somewhere special together. Knowing You makes me feel like I'm on a great adventure too. You do so many great things for me every day that are special. Thank You.

In Jesus' Name, Amen.

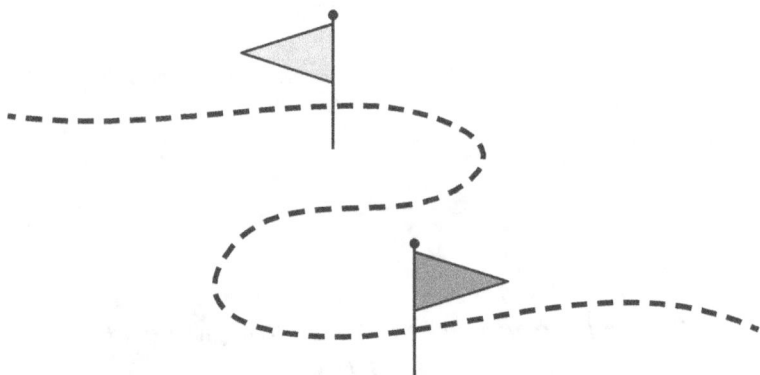

QUESTion: In what ways is life with God
an adventure?

_____

_____

_____

_____

_____

_____

_____

_____

_____

_____

_____

_____

_____

_____

_____

_____

"...on your wondrous works, I will meditate."
Psalm 145:5b

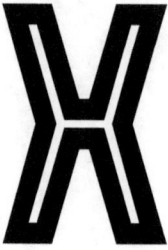

eXtol: TO GO CRAZY ABOUT; TO PRAISE WILDLY

Prayer: God, I don't always feel comfortable talking to others about You. I'm afraid my friends will make fun of me or think I'm weird. Can You give me courage today not to worry about what others think when I let them know You are in my life? I want to be able to tell them You help me not to be afraid. You help me not to worry about my dad or mom while he or she is deployed. If I can remember to talk about You today, I will feel less weird about doing that tomorrow.

In Jesus' Name, Amen.

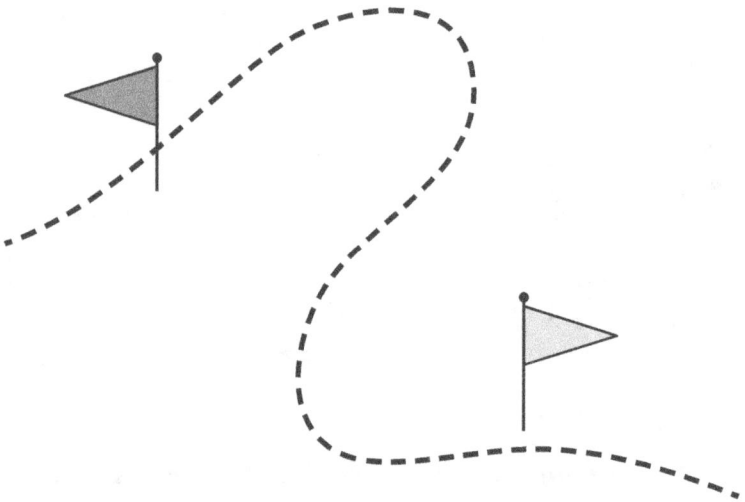

QUESTion: How will I tell someone about God today?

_____

_____

_____

_____

_____

_____

_____

_____

_____

_____

_____

_____

_____

_____

_____

"I will extol you, my God and King, and bless your name forever and ever." Psalm 145:1

YOURS: THING OR THINGS BELONGING TO GOD

Prayer: God, I have so many things: toys, games, a home, and those who love me. I have so much more than a lot of other people in the world. Some people are happy just to have a slice of bread to eat. But no matter how many things I have, You have a lot more. You own everything. You own the stars in the sky and all the sand on all the beaches. You own every piece of land and every animal on Earth. Everything is Yours, including me and my family. So I can trust everything to You and know that You will take care of us even when we are apart. This gives me peace.

In Jesus' Name, Amen.

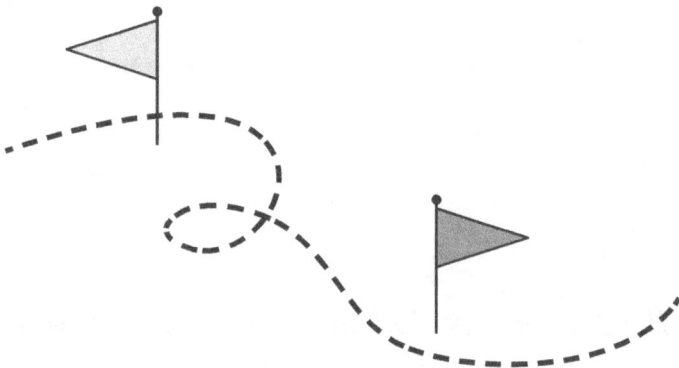

QUESTion: What worries you the most about this deployment? How can God help?

_____

_____

_____

_____

_____

_____

_____

_____

_____

_____

_____

_____

_____

_____

_____

_____

"All your works shall give thanks to you, O Lord, and all your saints shall bless you." Psalm 145:10

Z GAZE: TO LOOK; TO SEE

Prayer: God, when I go out at night and see all the stars in the sky, it's amazing. When I'm looking at the stars, I'm gazing into the bigness of the sky. And even if I had the largest telescope in the world, I still wouldn't see everything You've created. When I try to figure out how big You are, it's impossible. You are everywhere, even where my dad or mom is right now. So when I look at the sky, I know my dad or mom is looking at the same sky, too, and when we look to You, we're looking at the same God. That makes me feel good.

In Jesus' Name, Amen.

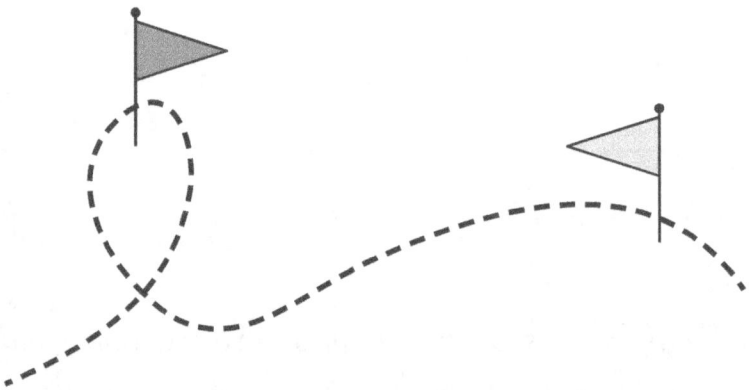

QUESTion: God is everywhere. Where do you see Him?

_____

_____

_____

_____

_____

_____

_____

_____

_____

_____

_____

_____

_____

_____

_____

_____

_____

"The eyes of all look to you." Psalm 145:15a

You have journeyed through the alphabet from A to Z, worshipping and praising God the Creator. You've been on a QUEST, a search for peace, happiness and safety while your dad or mom is deployed. You've shared your journey with God. You've learned He is always with you, looking out for you and your parents even though you are apart.

BUT, your journey doesn't finish with Z!

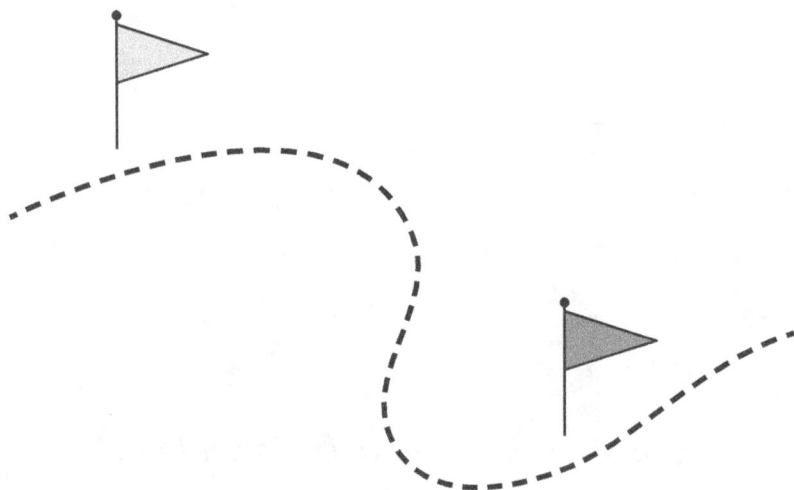

You have four more days
in your QUEST.

AND THEY ARE ALL ABOUT

GOD'S LOVE.

Learn: to find out how much God gave up for you

Did you know God loves you and has fantastic plans for you? You can talk to God about this...

Prayer: God, it's amazing that You love me so much and have great things planned for my life. I can't wait to see what will happen. This is Awesome! Just like the books that have a couple of different endings, I get to choose which one. I choose the one that makes You happy, the one where You are the main character and I walk beside You. Help me to remember You love me and are with me all the time.

In Jesus' Name, Amen.

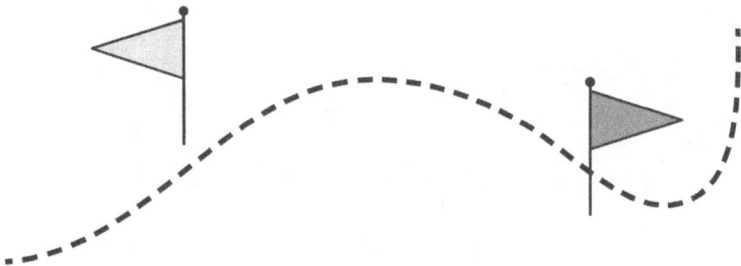

QUESTion: Make a list of people—with God at the top—who love you. What things do they love about you?

_____

_____

_____

_____

_____

_____

_____

_____

_____

_____

_____

_____

_____

_____

_____

_____

_____

"For God so loved the world, that He gave His only Son..." John 3:16a

ONE: TO HAVE A SINGLE CHOICE

All boys and girls and men and women have the same problem. They want to do whatever they want, and it doesn't matter if it's right or wrong. Have you ever done anything wrong, and you knew it was wrong when you were doing it? Well, it has been this way ever since God created Adam and Eve. People do things, thinking only of themselves. This is called being selfish, and it makes God so unhappy that He doesn't want to be friends with us.

Prayer: God, I know that I am selfish many times. I say and do bad things. I want stuff and don't share. I'm sometimes greedy and want to do things my way. I'm like the kid who takes his toys home and won't let other kids play with them because the kids won't do what he wants. Please help me to see when I am acting this way. I don't want You to be unhappy with me. I want to be Your friend.

In Jesus' Name, Amen.

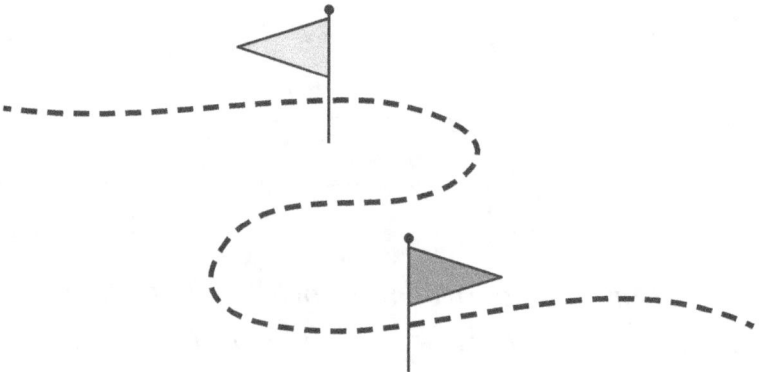

QUESTion: What does it mean to be God's friend?

_____

_____

_____

_____

_____

_____

_____

_____

_____

_____

_____

_____

_____

_____

_____

_____

_____

"...that whoever believes in Him should not perish but have eternal life." John 3:16b

saVe: TO TAKE CARE OF

Because all of us do bad things, God cannot be our friend. But He wants to be. In fact, that's why God made people! He wants lots of people to care for and love. So God came up with a plan so that He could be friends with us, even though we are not perfect like He is. His plan was to send His Son Jesus Christ to Earth to save us from our selfishness. That's why Jesus is called Savior. God says if anyone (like you) believes Jesus is God's Son and that Jesus died on the cross for all the bad things they do, then God will be their friend forever. He wants to be your friend forever.

Prayer: God, I love You and I thank You for sending Your Son Jesus to Earth to save me and all selfish people. Your plan is awesome and shows how much You really love us. I don't know anyone who would let their child die for someone else. Your love is so big. I don't get it, but I thank You for Your great love, and please help me never to forget it.

In Jesus' Name, Amen.

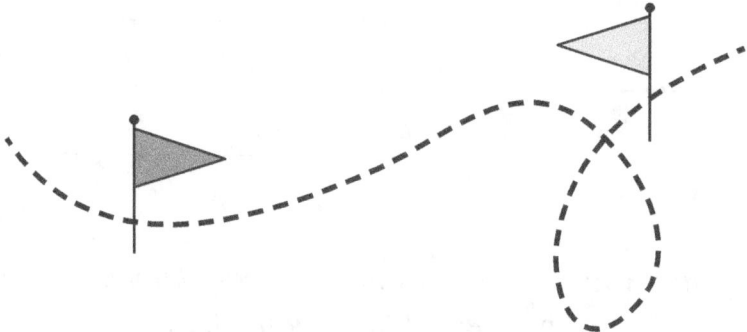

QUESTion: When you give up something important to you, it's called a sacrifice. How hard do you think it was for God to sacrifice His only Son so that you could be God's friend?

_____

_____

_____

_____

_____

_____

_____

_____

_____

_____

_____

_____

_____

_____

"For God did not send his Son into the world to condemn the world, but in order that the world might be saved through Him." John 3:17

Eternal: to last forever

Do you want to be sure you are God's friend? It's so simple. You know God loves you and has a fantastic plan for you. You also know that you are selfish and often do bad things. Yet God loves us so much that He sent His Son Jesus to die on the cross to save us from our selfishness. But knowing all this isn't enough. God wants you to talk to Him and tell Him that you know these things, and you want to change and let God rule your life so that you can become a better person. Just say the prayer below:

Prayer: God, I think and say and do bad things. I'm so sorry for making You unhappy. I want Jesus to be in my life, to walk beside me as my friend and to help me be the Christian kid You want me to be. I love You and I want to be Your friend.

In Jesus' Name, Amen.

Write down the date you prayed this prayer so you'll always know this is the day you asked God into your heart …

_____

QUESTion: How does it feel to know you will live forever with God?

_____

_____

_____

_____

_____

_____

_____

_____

_____

_____

_____

_____

_____

_____

_____

"...whoever does what is true comes to the light, so that it may be clearly seen that his deeds have been carried out in God." John 3:21

CONGRATULATIONS!

You have made the most important decision of your life.

You are now part of God's family.

YOU MAY THINK THE QUEST IS FINISHED, BUT YOUR JOURNEY WITH GOD WILL CARRY ON FOREVER.

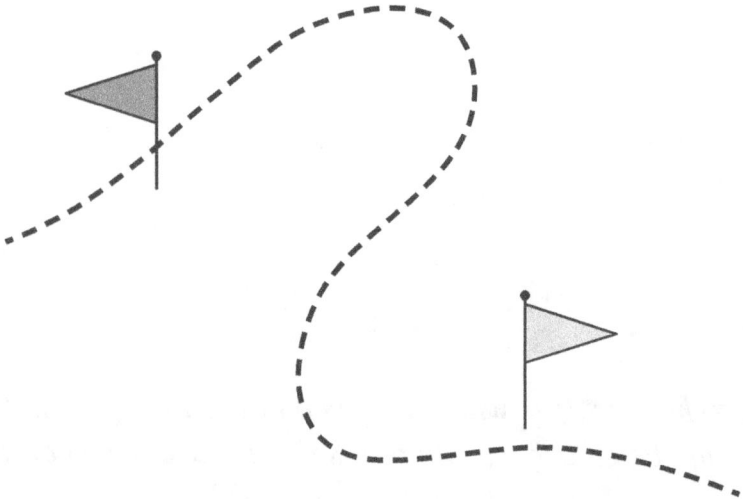

The adventure continues . . .

QUEST SCRIPTURE VERSES

Awesome: "They shall speak of the might of your awesome deeds." Psalm 145:6a

Bless: "Every day I will bless you." Psalm 145:2a

Commend: "One generation shall commend your works to another, and shall declare your mighty acts." Psalm 145:4

Dominion: "Your kingdom is an everlasting kingdom, and your dominion endures throughout all generations." Psalm 145:13

Exalt: "...to make known to the children of man your mighty deeds." Psalm 145:12a

Forever: "...and bless your name forever and ever." Psalm 145:1b

Greatness: "Great is the Lord, and greatly to be praised, and his greatness is unsearchable." Psalm 145:3

Holy: "...and let all flesh bless his holy name forever and ever." Psalm 145:21b

I will: "...I will declare your greatness." Psalm 145:6b

Joyful: [With great joy] "My mouth will speak the praise of the Lord." Psalm 145:21a

Kingdom: "They shall speak of the glory of your kingdom, and tell of your power." Psalm 145:11

Lord: "The Lord is good to all." Psalm 145:9a

Merciful: "The Lord is gracious and merciful, slow to anger and abounding in steadfast love." Psalm 145:8

Near: "The Lord is near to all who call on him, to all who call on him in truth." Psalm 145:18

One: "One generation shall commend your works to another, and shall declare your mighty acts." Psalm 145:4

Praise: "...and praise your name forever and ever." Psalm 145:2b

Quality: "The Lord is good to all." Psalm 145:9a

Righteous: "The Lord is righteous in all his ways and kind in all his works." Psalm 145:17

Splendor: "...the glorious splendor of your kingdom." Psalm 145:12b

Truth: "The Lord is near to all who call on him, to all who call on him in truth." Psalm 145:18

Upholds: "The Lord upholds all who are falling." Psalm 145:14a

eVerlasting: "Your kingdom is an everlasting kingdom." Psalm 145:13a

Wondrous: "...on your wondrous works, I will meditate." Psalm 145:5b

eXtol: "I will extol you, my God and King, and bless your name forever and ever." Psalm 145:1

Yours: "All your works shall give thanks to you, O Lord, and all your saints shall bless you." Psalm 145:10

gaZe: "The eyes of all look to you." Psalm 145:15a

NOTES AND COMMENTS